Tom Semark, on the last
occasion _ _ _ _

Frances.

3 June 1959.

THE LIE OF THE LAND

Showing the lake with the island, and a corner of Blenheim Palace on the left. On the right, over the bridge, is the site of Woodstock Manor House

INTRODUCTION TO

Woodstock

BY

J. M. SHELMERDINE

WITH DRAWINGS BY

IAIN MACNAB

THE SAMSON PRESS, WOODSTOCK

1951

NOTE

This does not pretend to be a complete or scholarly history of Woodstock; still less to make any new contribution to the subject. It contains, in fact, but a very small part of what is already known, and is simply an attempt to put into a convenient form, for visitors and others, an outline of the events which have taken place in this historic town.

Serious students of history will complain that I have simplified too much and explained too much. The answer is that I have had in mind those visitors who, in the course of busy lives, have forgotten a good deal of the history they learnt at school, as well as those, almost as numerous, who come from parts of the world where English history is little studied.

The two chief sources upon which I have drawn are *The Early History of Woodstock Manor*, by Edward Marshall, and *Chronicles of the Royal Borough of Woodstock*, by Adolphus Ballard. A guide to the town is published under the auspices of the Corporation, and a guide to Blenheim Palace by the Blenheim Estate Office.

I should like to take this opportunity of thanking the many people who have given me encouragement, help, advice, and the loan of books.

Woodstock   J. M. SHELMERDINE
1951

Introduction to Woodstock

⚜ I ⚜

'What a lovely little place it is,' said the visitor to Woodstock, stopping in Park Street one warm spring evening to look around her. 'And so peaceful ! One feels that nothing much could ever happen here.'

She was wrong. A great deal has happened here; and those events, wider in variety and more highly coloured than commonly falls to the lot of so small a town, have been going on for longer than anyone would care to estimate. 'Tyme out of anie man's remembrance' is a phrase that keeps cropping up in Woodstock records.

The history of Woodstock begins in what is now Blenheim Park, which, until the early eighteenth century, was known as the Park or Chase of Woodstock. If the visitor will walk up Park Street and pass through the Triumphal Arch which now forms the main entrance to Blenheim, he will see before him one of the loveliest landscapes in England, a scene deliberately laid out to astonish the beholder. Before him lies the lake with its tufted island, fringed with dogwood and plumed with poplars; beyond it, Blenheim Palace, the whole backed by fold upon fold of trees, clothed in every shade of summer green, and lit, if there be sunlight, by gleams from the wide waters of the lake beyond the bend. The vista, like a transformation scene, looks infinitely deeper than it really is.

In front of the Palace a road crosses the lake at its narrowest point, carried by a magnificent stone bridge. As we stand inside the Triumphal Arch and look to the right of the bridge, we see a tree-crowned plateau jutting out into the lake towards us. Here, for six centuries or more, stood a country residence of the kings of England, known as the Manor House of Woodstock.

In the lifetime of the Manor House the scene was very different. Blenheim Palace had not been built; there was no lake and no bridge. The River Glyme, which crosses the main Oxford to Chipping Norton road at the foot of the hill between Woodstock and the separate village of Old Woodstock, and enters the Park at this point now to form the lake, wandered in those days past the mansioned-crowned plateau through lush water-meadows. Visitors to the Manor House crossed this marsh-land by a raised causeway of which the only remaining trace is that small oval-shaped island, pointing like a finger towards the deserted site, and now called after Queen Elizabeth.

How skilled designers in the eighteenth century changed the land-scape to make a worthier approach to Blenheim Palace is no part of the Woodstock story. We must keep in mind that, throughout the centuries of Royal Woodstock, with which we have to deal, this now famous prospect offered only a view of meadow, stream, and marsh, with the wild woods beyond, and a low hill topped by a building, at first, perhaps, a mere hunting-box, but later a vast turreted pile of stone, an accretion of rooms great and small, of chapels and gate-house, of courtyards and formal garden: a palace not built to the design of a known architect, but one that was many centuries in growing.

The name Woodstock means a stockaded settlement in a wood, and at the beginning of our story, that is before the Norman Con-quest, the whole of Oxfordshire was largely forest, except in the fertile river valleys, where flocks of sheep already pastured, and the swampy wastes of Otmoor. The five forests of Wychwood, Corn-bury, Woodstock, Stowood, and Shotover were almost continuous, and only a few sparsely populated hamlets intervened. To the hunting Norman kings such land was irresistible, but we know that already before the Conquest, Woodstock was a place of occasional residence for Anglo-Saxon royalty.

Before the coming of the Saxons there were Romano-British settlements in the district. A Roman road, Akeman Street, crosses the northern part of Blenheim Park, and the remains of several large villas, or Roman country houses, have been excavated in the neigh-bourhood. There seems no foundation for the legend that the Manor House itself was built on the site of a Roman villa, for the Saxons, who invaded Britain in the fifth century and destroyed Romano-British civilization, wrecked and burnt the towns and villas and massacred the inhabitants, after which they understandably tried to avoid reoccupying the same sites.

Another legend tells us that Woodstock was a royal residence in King Alfred's days, and that here he translated the *Consolations of Philosophy* of Boethius, somewhere about the year 890. Dr. Robert Plot, first Keeper of the Ashmolean Museum, writing in 1677, claimed to have seen Alfred's manuscript, but it is now missing and the story cannot be verified.

With Ethelred the Redeless (978–1016) we are on firmer ground. Ethelred held a Council at Woodstock, and issued a decree for the maintenance of peace 'for the whole nation, at Woodstock, in the land of the Mercians, according to the law of the English'. Extracts can be found in Anglo-Saxon charters, and there occurs this sentence: 'But let God's law be henceforth zealously loved, by word and deed,

then will God soon be merciful to this nation.' Fine words to be the
first that emerge from Woodstock, nearly a thousand years ago,
though we may think that Ethelred was the wrong person to utter
them.

A Witenagemot in the forest at Woodstock would suggest a
building large enough to house both king and Witan, but it is not
likely that Ethelred's house survived by long the Norman Conquest.
It was probably built of wood. The Saxons used stone for ecclesi-
astical rather than domestic purposes, and in any case the house at
Woodstock was not Ethelred's permanent home. The great wooden
halls of the Anglo-Saxon noblemen were doubtless just as comfortable
as the grimmer stone castles of their conquerors. The Viking
invaders had brought with them a skill in ship-building which was to
become part of the English heritage, and which, applied on land,
gave builders a mastery in the use of wood. A development of this
may be seen in the elaborate timber roofs of a later age.

Woodstock is described in Domesday Book as one of the 'demesne
forests of the king', forests being land reserved for hunting, inhabited
and cultivated merely on sufferance, or not at all. To the Anglo-
Saxons, hunting had been a pleasure rather than an organized sport,
and there had been little legislation to protect the game, which was
well able to protect itself against the thinly scattered peasantry, as
the forest slowly yielded to their clearings. With the Conquest,
Norman forest law and forest courts were transplanted to England,
a source of oppression to all who lived within their jurisdiction.
In early Norman times, as many as sixty-nine forests belonged to the
Crown, comprising about a third of the kingdom. Within their
bounds, forest law deprived the inhabitants of many essential and
ordinary rights, and inflicted atrocious penalties on wrongdoers. The
poaching of deer was punished by mutilation or death.

The third of the Norman kings, Henry I (1100–35), the youngest
son of the Conqueror, built, or rebuilt, the Manor House at Woodstock. Built, because there is no means of knowing on what site the
house of Ethelred stood, while that of Henry's hunting-lodge is
unquestioned, since its history has been continuous into relatively
modern times. He also enclosed within a stone wall a park seven
miles in circumference, said to be the first walled park, and stocked
it with wild beasts: lions, leopards, camels, and even a porcupine,
which a chronicler described as covered with sharp quills, 'which it
shot at the dogs that hunted it'. To Henry I is also attributed the
founding of Old Woodstock on the hill-side beyond the Glyme. He
spent a good deal of time at the Manor House, and a charter by

which he granted a mill to the Abbot of Abingdon is dated: 'At Wdestoc in the park, in the year in which the king gave his daughter to the Roman Emperor.' That was probably 1110, the year of the betrothal, so that a considerable amount of building must have been done here in the first decade of Henry's reign. An able ruler, whose reign brought order to Norman England, Henry had a leaning towards scholarship, and it may be that what drew him to build at Woodstock was the proximity not only of the forest of Wychwood, which merged into his Chase of Woodstock, but also of the learned men who were beginning to gather at Oxford, long before the University could be said to exist.

Henry's only son had been drowned at sea, and the two claimants to his throne were his daughter Matilda, now widow of the Emperor, and his nephew Stephen. In the grim war that broke out between them, Woodstock was held for Matilda, until her escape from Oxford Castle, cloaked in white, on foot over the snow. The reign of Stephen is a period without equal in our history for lawlessness, bloodshed, and oppression; the feudal barons, uncontrolled, multiplied their castles, from which they harried the land with pillage and torture. This devastated England, from which law and justice had disappeared, was the heritage of Matilda's son, Henry II (1154–89).

2

Henry II was one of the greatest of medieval monarchs, and few at any time have done such lasting work for England. The son of Matilda by her second husband, Geoffrey, Count of Anjou, he ruled over a vast empire from the Cheviots to the Pyrenees, and was a power to reckon with in European, let alone English, affairs. He put a stop to the anarchy, razed the baronial castles, and set afoot a reform of the law.

His domestic affairs, on the other hand, were unfortunate. His wife, Eleanor, duchess in her own right of Aquitaine, whom he had married to enlarge his empire and further his claim to England, was thirteen years his senior and already divorced from the French king. Her life-story is a saga on its own. A woman of ability, energy, and vitality, she was dissolute, vindictive, cruel, and scheming. Estranged from Henry—himself as faithless—she incited their sons into open rebellion against him, for which he kept her in prison for sixteen years. She outlived him to be a doughty old warrior of eighty, who had ably held England for the crusading Richard against his brother

John, and who, by an odd turn of character and fortune, came to be known to the English as 'good Queen Eleanor'.

Henry was a tireless hunter, and some of his most important Councils were held in hunting-lodges, of which Woodstock was perhaps the favourite. Here, at all events, he brought his mistress Rosamond Clifford, the 'Fair Rosamund' of ballad and story, for whom he is said to have built a 'bower' or dwelling-place outside the walls of the Manor House, and protected by a complicated maze. The legend goes that Queen Eleanor, arriving at Woodstock unbidden, saw a ball of silk attached to the king's spur, and following it to its source through the labyrinth, she confronted Rosamund, whom she poisoned with a cup of wine.

Without suggesting that Eleanor was incapable of poisoning a rival, we note that there are other and more prosaic versions of the story. One is, of course, that Henry virtuously dismissed Rosamund on his marriage and that she retired in penitence to the convent at Godstow, where she was undoubtedly buried. Traces of this nunnery may still be seen on the bank of the Thames, opposite the Trout Inn. The dates, however, conflict. Henry had married two years before his accession, and it was as king that he kept Rosamund at Woodstock.

A third version is that Henry tired of Rosamund and sent her to Godstow, and a fourth is that she died a natural death at Woodstock. The only certain fact is that Rosamund was buried at Godstow. It was no unusual thing for a great lady to be buried in the precincts of a nunnery, to which money would be given that Masses might be said for her soul, and we need not on that account assume that Rosamund had become a nun, or even an inmate. She might, moreover, have become an inmate without being a penitent. English nunneries in the Middle Ages were not all refuges for the poor, nor were they restricted to women of religious vocation. They provided a harbour for superfluous ladies, whose families sometimes had good reason to want them out of sight. Generations of bishops waged war against the lack of discipline in English nunneries, the fashions in clothes, pet dogs and monkeys, and trains of servants.

Such a bishop was St. Hugh of Lincoln. In 1191 he visited the nunnery of Godstow, which was in his diocese. He observed a tomb in the choir, furnished with lights and a silken pall, and, hearing that it was Rosamund Clifford's, he ordered the body to be taken up and reburied outside the chapel. He was obeyed, but after his death the remains of Rosamund were returned to the choir, where they rested until the Dissolution. Plainly, therefore, the bishop did not regard

B

the lady as a penitent, and it may be true that she was still the king's mistress when death overtook her at Woodstock.

Yet another version tells that Rosamund was secretly married to Henry before he met Eleanor, and that she was a willing prisoner at Woodstock out of love for her husband, whom she did not know to be the king. This would make Henry's marriage to Eleanor bigamous, and render illegitimate a whole line of English monarchs. But it does not tally with the anecdote about the bishop.

One would like to know more about Rosamund, who is a vital link in Woodstock history. About a hundred years later, sworn evidence was given by a jury of Woodstock men that the King Henry le Veyl (Henry II) 'often resided in his Manor of Wodestock for the love of a certain woman named Rosamund; and at the same time there was a certain unused plot without the Park of the said Manor, and because the men of the King were lodged too far from his Manor aforesaid, the same lord the king granted divers portions of land of the demesne to divers men for the purpose of building hostelries thereon for the use of the men of the said king.' They added that Henry had established a weekly market on Tuesdays, to which his son John, 'moved with exceeding pity because of the poverty of the said vill', had added a fair lasting three days at the feast of St. Matthew.

Woodstock, in brief, was built on about forty acres of waste ground at the Park gate, a fact that has restricted its confines throughout its history. In its unambitious beginnings it simply provided a lodging for the retinue of the king. That the land was granted to a relatively large number of small-holders, sufficiently explains their poverty.

The first difference of opinion between Henry II and Thomas Becket, Archbishop of Canterbury, took place at a Council at Woodstock, when high words passed between king and prelate. During their last fatal quarrel, the archbishop made two more visits to the Manor House, and on the second occasion was repulsed from the door.

Another odd scene occurred here between the king and Bishop Hugh of Lincoln. The bishop had infuriated Henry by excommunicating the latter's chief forester, and, being at Dorchester, was summoned to Woodstock. The king gave him no greeting and offered him no seat. The bishop made room for himself among the noblemen near the king. To hide his anger the king sent for a needle and thread, and began sewing a rag round one of his fingers, which had been wounded. The bishop waited for a while, and then spoke: 'How like you are to your relatives at Falaise !' whereupon the king threw himself on the ground in a paroxysm of fury. The allusion was to the mother of the Conqueror, a low-born woman of Falaise in Normandy, the inhabitants of which were famous for dressing skins. The king, who had evidently been sulking, recovered quickly after his explosion, and the differences were discussed and settled.

Henry's chief legislative acts were comprised in his Assizes, of which one, The Assize of Woodstock, set out the forest code in all its stringency. To such Councils a vast number of people were summoned, and the need for hostelries at Woodstock becomes still more plain. The Manor House itself had grown in Henry's time. It contained a chapel, later described as a round chapel, big enough for a royal wedding, when William the Lion, King of Scotland, married a relative of the English king, amid festivities lasting for four days.

3

Both Richard I and the infamous John came to Woodstock during their reigns. The latter is said to have been a frequent visitor, and to have stayed here shortly after signing Magna Carta. His pious and ineffectual son, Henry III (1216–72), was a great builder and, besides repairing and enlarging the Manor House, he is credited with some building in Woodstock itself. Of the origins of Woodstock Church, nothing has been recorded. It was never a parish church, but was, and still is, a chapel of ease to the parochial church of Bladon. It was probably built at the same time as the beginnings of the town, as would appear from the remains of a chevron-encircled Norman door on the south side. In 1279 it already had a bell-tower and a burial-ground, while the font is of the next century. A chapel which could provide for baptism and burial had the right to be regarded as a parish church, but it never was so. Ruthless restorations have robbed the church of its beauty, but on the south side there are still some early English windows and five arches supported on round pillars, the capitals carved with foliage, and heads that are plainly portraits. The crowned head with a foolish expression is alleged to be that of Henry III, and the work has been attributed to his time.

Henry III built a chapel in the Manor House, dedicated to St. Edward, and known as the Queen's Chapel, or New Chapel, the older one being the King's Chapel. There is also a mention in his reign of the Chapel of the High Tower, and on another occasion of 'all the king's chapels'.

STONE HEADS OF THE 13TH CENTURY, WOODSTOCK CHURCH

In 1256 the king received at Woodstock King Alexander III of Scotland and his wife, Henry's own daughter. 'The nobles', says Matthew Paris, 'had assembled there in immense numbers by the king's command, and when they were all present, there were reckoned many thousand men and many horses, and no city, not even the Royal Manor of Woodstock, where they were collected, was able to receive them. Moreover, the City of Oxford and the rural vills around were filled with guests. And from this place they set out towards London by different roads, that there might be no want of provisions for so great a multitude.' Considering the hardships of travel in those days, one would suppose that the accommodation in and around Woodstock would be reserved for the great: the lower the rank, the farther from the centre. As it was August, the servants probably camped in the park. Then the departing train of guests divides into separate snakes, eating their several ways across the countryside, leaving depleted barns and farmyards in their wake. Rich people travelled not only with luggage, horses, and very necessary men-at-arms, but with bedding, cooking utensils and plate, and a host of servants to attend to these matters.

Minor events at the Manor House during this reign included the marriage of two penniless maidens of Provence to two reluctant English youths of noble birth, and a hair-raising attempt on the king's life, foiled by a pious Scotswoman.

In the reign of Henry's great and legal-minded son, Edward I (1272–1307), detailed inquiries were made into certain matters of local administration. A jury in each territorial division or 'hundred' gave witness to a commission appointed by the king, and the result was set down in documents now known as the 'Rolls of the Hundreds'.

These tell us a great deal about medieval Woodstock. In 1279, when a survey was made, there were 137 houses, but apparently only 108 householders, suggesting that some people held more than one house. The population has been assessed at about 540 inhabitants. Rents varied from 18d. paid by John atte Green for a house opposite the stone cross, to 2d. paid by Walter the Miller for one opposite the shambles. Some householders paid no money rent: Agnes Batecok tenanted a house in return for supplying the king with 1 lb. of cinnamon yearly, and maintaining one lamp in the king's chapel. Such rents sound preposterously low, but so would the incomes out of which they were paid, and the standard of life was by no means high. Woodstock was already well supplied with craftsmen and tradesmen: we note Henry le Yronmongare, John le Deyere, Thomas le Harper, Jordan le Nappere, Stephen le Parchemyner,

John le Wymplere (whose work is perhaps represented on the carved heads of the women in Woodstock Church), as well as a tailor, a carpenter, a tanner, a turner, a smith, a weaver, a potter, a chapman, and a number of parkers and marshals. The smallest villages had to be self-sufficient for their ordinary needs, while Woodstock was already accounted of importance enough to send two representatives to the Parliaments of 1302 and 1305. By 1377 the population had dropped by about half, probably on account of the Black Death, which wiped out a third to half of the inhabitants of the country.

Two of Edward I's children by his second wife, Margaret of France, 'good withouten lack', were born at the Manor House. The first of them, Edmund of Woodstock, was put to death in horrible circumstances shortly after the murder of his half-brother, Edward II, when the latter's widow and her lover, Mortimer, established a brief rule of terror. These two were said to have lived uproariously at Woodstock, but, though the Manor had been made over to this extremely unpleasant queen, there is no evidence that she occupied the house. From now on the Manor appears to have formed part of the dowry of the queens.

With Edward III (1327-77) we come to something of a golden age in the Manor's long history. His queen was Philippa of Hainault, of whom Froissart said that she was 'beloved of God and all men'. Woodstock seems to have been her favourite country residence, and it saw the birth of several of her children, including her eldest son, Edward the Black Prince. We know that he was born on Friday, 15 June 1330, at 10 a.m., his nurse being Joan de Oxford, and his rocker Maud Plumpton.

The visitor to Woodstock will probably be told that the Black Prince was born in an ancient house still standing in Old Woodstock, on the right side of the hill going towards Chipping Norton, now known as the Manor House of Old Woodstock. There is no evidence that the queen left the palace to give birth to her child in Old Woodstock, while the absurdity of the tale that this house formed part of the royal Manor House is evident on topographical grounds alone. Two things seem to have led to the confusion: first, that this house was, by tradition, an occasional residence of the Black Prince in later life—it was known for generations as Praunce's Place, or Prince's Palace—and second, the name of Manor House, by which it goes today, causing it to be wrongly identified with the vanished palace of the kings. The house now standing on this site in Old Woodstock is mainly Tudor, though parts are still older. Its most interesting feature is an ancient chimney hollowed from a solid block of carved stone, with slits to let out the smoke and a pierced conical top.

In the year of the Black Prince's birth the Court was at Woodstock for over three months. Two of the king's daughters were subsequently born here, as well as his sixth son, Thomas. To celebrate this last event a great tournament was held at the Manor House, which must have been one of the most brilliant scenes in its history. But Thomas of Woodstock was as ill starred as Edmund of Woodstock his great-uncle, and came to as unpleasant an end.

The Manor House by this time was a rambling old mansion. The bleak fortresses in which the Norman barons had spent their lives were giving way to more comfortable houses, less essentially planned for self-defence, though they still presented blank walls, pierced with narrow shot-holes, to the outside world, and a drawbridge approach. Inside the courtyard, however, were larger windows to let in the light, and there were fireplaces from which the smoke went up through the thicknesses of the walls. More rooms gave greater privacy; there were tapestries on the walls and a formal garden. The occupants of manor-houses spent their leisure in deer-hunting and hawking, or tilting in tournaments before a gallery of ladies; their serious pursuits were war and local administration. The horses on which they rode to the hunt were still heavy, being bred to carry a knight in full armour at a trot. Men's costume was becoming flashy: tight-fitting hose, often parti-coloured, and contrasting short jackets, made of costly stuff and glittering with jewels. Sleeves hung to the ground and the points of shoes sometimes had to be chained to the waist. Those who still clung to the long medieval gown now tended to wear it trailing behind them, sweeping the filthy rushes on the floor. Both men and women wore high hats of eccentric shape and fantastic colour.

※ 4 ※

The most persistent of legends about Woodstock, which has been repeated in every age, is that Geoffrey Chaucer was born here. It is a pity that Woodstock must reject the claim to being the birthplace of the first great English poet, the author of the *Canterbury Tales*, but doubtless Chaucer, during the years of his employment by Edward III, often had occasion to come here, and there are reasonable grounds for thinking that Thomas Chaucer, who had a great deal to do with Woodstock, was the poet's son.

The poet, who was almost certainly born in London, the son of a vintner, distinguished himself in the service of the Crown. He was sent abroad on several confidential missions by the king, from whom he received many marks of favour, including a pension. He also drew a pension from John of Gaunt, Duke of Lancaster, the king's fourth son. In 1366 there is mention of a lady called Philippa Chaucer, in attendance on Queen Philippa of Hainault, who is believed to have been the poet's wife. She has less certainly been identified with Philippa Roet, also of Hainault, whose sister became John of Gaunt's third wife, after having been his children's governess. This would explain the special favour shown by John of Gaunt to Chaucer and his wife.

Returning to Woodstock: the last house on the right in Park Street, near the entrance to Blenheim, is called Chaucer's House, and has been so called since the time of Queen Elizabeth. Before that it was called Hanwell House. A house on this site, in the early fifteenth century, belonged to a Thomas Chaucer; and if Philippa Roet was the poet's wife, then Thomas was his son, as will presently appear. Thomas Chaucer distinguished himself in a very different way from Geoffrey. Like the poet, he sat in Parliament—he was a Speaker of the House of Commons—but he was not a poet, and he died a very rich man.

In 1411, about eleven years after the poet's death, Henry IV's queen, Joanna of Navarre, granted to Thomas Chaucer, in return for services rendered, the farm of the Manor of Woodstock, to hold during his life. Thomas, through his wife Matilda Burghersh, already possessed estates at Ewelme, near Wallingford, and also in Berkshire, but this is the first appearance of the name Chaucer in Woodstock, and even now there is no mention of a specific house. Only in 1438 does evidence appear that Matilda Chaucer owned 'in Wodestocke one tenement with garden adjacent called Hanwell, situate by the Park'.

Thomas Chaucer was buried at Ewelme, and the arms of Roet are on his tomb, but not the arms that had been borne by Geoffrey Chaucer. It seems, however, that a Thomas Chaucer succeeded to the poet's last dwelling at Westminster, which surely need not be another coincidence. Nothing would seem to be gained by wilfully multiplying the Geoffreys and Thomases surnamed Chaucer !

Briefly to wind up the story of Chaucer's House: Alice, the daughter and heir of Sir Thomas and Lady Chaucer, married for her third husband, the Duke of Suffolk. Together they built the church, grammar school, and almshouses at Ewelme, which still stand in unspoilt beauty. The Duke was beheaded, and when his family died out their estate still included 'two messuages' at Woodstock. A newly created Duke of Suffolk, Charles Brandon, apparently became possessed of the property of his forerunners, for in a document of the reign of Queen Elizabeth the house, by that time belonging to the Crown, is referred to as 'Chaucer's House, parcel of our lands acquired of Charles, late Duke of Suffolk'.

The old house was rebuilt in the eighteenth century. It was owned for several generations by a family named Prior, and at the beginning of the present century was the home of Sir William Nicholson, the artist, whose maternal grandparents were Priors of Chaucer's House.

※ 5 ※

The year 1453 was a notable one. It saw the capture of Constantinople by the Turks, and the consequent flight of Greek scholars westwards, bringing with them a new kind of learning that was gradually to change the outlook of the western world. The Renaissance was to take a long time to reach England, still an outpost on the edge of the known world; but here in 1453 came the end of the Hundred Years War with France, the end of an ambition to found an English empire in Europe, clearing the way for an expansion as yet wholly unforeseen.

To Woodstock, a small remote spot on the map of England, 24th May of this same year was of the highest importance, as the date of its first Charter of Incorporation. Before this Charter, granted by Henry VI (1422–61), Woodstock already had its independent government by tradition, as is proved by certain documents of much earlier date, witnessed by mayors of Woodstock. And now, fearing lest their liberties should be curtailed 'for want of being set down and expressed', the inhabitants besought the king to establish their

c

position. The Charter stated that the king's beloved tenants of the Vill of New Woodstock, 'which is of the ancient demesne of our

crown', had represented to him the liberties and customs which they had already enjoyed 'for a long time past', and which they wished to have put on a legal basis. The Charter therefore declared that the tenants, residents, and inhabitants, with their heirs and successors should be free burgesses, that they should have a Merchant Guild and Guildhall, and enjoy the same liberties and free customs as the burgesses of New Windsor.

Only members of the Merchant Guild were to trade within the town. The new body corporate was given the name of the Mayor and Commonalty of the Borough of New Woodstock, and a seal was granted—which is still in the possession of the Corporation. A Mayor and Sergeant-at-Mace were to be elected by the freemen, but as yet no other officers were mentioned. A Portmouth Court, or independent Borough Court, was provided for, while County Sheriffs and Justices, or Crown officers, were forbidden to interfere in the free government of the town. The king granted to the Mayor and Commonalty the possession of the whole borough, and in addition 'a certain pool or marsh adjoining the town, and known as Le Pool', for which they had to pay rent. By this grant the rents of the houses accrued to the town instead of to the Crown. The town gained other privileges. It was to keep the fines and forfeitures and other perquisites hitherto the king's; it was to have the assay and

MEMORIAL BRASS TO
RICHARD BAILLY, HABER-
DASHER OF LONDON
AND CHAPMAN OF
WOODSTOCK, DIED 1441

assize of bread and beer and other victuals (that is, to establish the quality and price), and, in addition to the fair at the feast of St. Matthew, to have a five-day fair at the feast of St. Mary Magdalene, who is the patron saint of Woodstock Church. The inhabitants of the borough might bequeath their property to whomsoever they would, and no inhabitant was to be taken into serfdom—a highly valued privilege. Moreover, the borough was exempt 'for ever' from sending Burgesses to Parliament. This sounds an odd franchise, but in those days the expense and inconvenience of sending representatives to Westminster far outweighed the benefits, and to those elected the honour was so unwelcome that they sometimes absconded to avoid it. Woodstock's 'perpetual' exemption came to an end in the reign of Mary Tudor.

The gentle and pious King Henry VI was a benefactor to Woodstock Church as well as to the town. Being but a chapel to Bladon, two miles away, the church lacked services commensurate with the population, and owing to the poverty of the inhabitants had fallen into disrepair. Perpetual poverty was the condition of medieval Woodstock, for land was still the source of wealth, and of land it had far too little. Yet beyond Woodstock lies the beginning of the Cotswolds, already a prosperous region of sheep-farming, and the wool it produced was considered the best in Europe, to all parts of which it was exported.

A few months before the date of the Charter, 'in consideration of the great poverty' of Woodstock, the king granted letters patent for the establishment of a chantry, with a chaplain who would hold daily services and pray for himself and the queen during their lifetime and for their souls in perpetuity. This may have been the Chantry of Our Lady, which came to possess a good deal of property in the neighbourhood of Woodstock Church. Later, when Protestantism had triumphed, prayers for the dead were regarded as superstitious, chantries were abolished, and their lands seized and sold by the Crown. In the report made on Woodstock chantries at that time, the Chantry of Our Lady was described as founded by the inhabitants, no mention being made of Henry VI; so if it is the identical chantry, we must conclude that he merely gave the licence, and that people had to be found to put up the money. As late as 1535 a yearly payment was agreed upon by the Mayor and Council for a priest to pray for the founder, the benefactors, and the donors of lands to the chantry. The same report mentions a second chantry, called the chantry of St. Margaret, founded by one Edward Croft at an unspecified date, for a priest 'to synge and praye for all Chrysten souls'. Founding a chantry usually meant giving, raising, or leaving money for Masses to be said 'in perpetuity', and often a small chapel was provided in the gift to contain the founder's tomb.

In the reign of Henry VI his uncle, Humphrey, Duke of Gloucester, had a grant for life of the Manor of Woodstock. He was one of the earliest English patrons of Renaissance scholars, and his gift of 'Duke Humphrey's Library' to the University of Oxford formed the beginning of the Bodleian collection.

The feudal aristocracy of medieval England extinguished itself in the Wars of the Roses. To this day, people take sides in the Civil War of Charles I's reign, to the point of writing angry letters to the newspapers. But the dynastic fight-to-the-death between the Houses of York and Lancaster and their adherents, in which no apparent principle was at stake, means to us no more than 'the lion and the unicorn fighting for the crown'. Even at the time, the mass of the people looked on with indifference, and tried not to be involved in the outburst of savagery which afflicted their 'betters', unemployed after a hundred years of fighting in France. Poor Henry VI was deposed. Edward IV (1461–83), who supplanted him, confirmed the Woodstock Charter at the inhabitants' request. The earliest existing rent-roll of the borough dates from this reign. It shows that in 1469 there were at least 110 houses, among which is specifically mentioned the George Inn, now the 'Marlborough Arms'. Expenses include 9s. for repairs to the stocks and ducking-stool.

On one occasion Edward IV came to Woodstock with his English queen, her mother, and other relatives, and they paid a state visit to Oxford to see the new buildings of Magdalen College. They arrived after sunset, riding in procession, with runners going before them carrying torches—presumably in relays. They were met at the North Gate by the Chancellor of the University, who 'happened to be' the queen's brother, and spent the night at Magdalen, returning to Woodstock the following day.

This same king gave great offence by extending the limits of Wychwood Forest 'to the injury of the country', a wrong that was redressed by the next reigning king, Richard III.

❧ 6 ❧

The Wars of the Roses lasted, on and off, for twenty years, until Henry Tudor, a Welsh gentleman, descended from the House of Lancaster through John of Gaunt and that third wife who may have been Chaucer's sister-in-law, won the Battle of Bosworth, assumed the crown, and reconciled his opponents by marrying into the House of York. When Henry VII succeeded, his kingdom was lawless and his finances threadbare; when he died, England was prosperous and at rest, and the House of Tudor secure upon the throne. This result he achieved through his own ability and prestige, and through the hearty desire of the people to see the King's Peace restored.

Woodstock Manor came back into favour with Henry VII (1485–1509), and he did a great deal of rebuilding there. He seems to have altered the house and rebuilt the gatehouse. Large rooms and galleries with wide lattice windows were typical of early Tudor times, the fortress aspect of their mansions receding still farther into the background. The commonest form of Tudor manor-house was an enclosed court, entered through an enormous turreted gatehouse. Such was the gatehouse built at Woodstock by Henry VII, and though, on the causeway side, the Manor appears to have retained much of its old outline, Henry, according to John Aubrey, altered the southern and western aspects, where his initials were displayed in the windows. In one year he spent £845 on the house, a large sum in those days.

Like his Plantagenet ancestor, Henry VII conducted some of the business of the realm from his hunting-lodges. In 1507 the Spanish Ambassador, seeking an interview with the king who was hunting from forest to forest, arranged to meet him at 'a town which is called Woodstock, 55 miles distant from London. He informed me that he would be there on the 26th of July. . . . When I knew this, I bought the horses necessary for me and my servants. . . . I was obliged to buy ten horses and all the outfit needful for me and my servants, in addition to what I and they had already. That was necessary, because the king was accompanied by the ambassadors from the Pope, the King of the Romans, the King of France, from Flanders, Denmark and Scotland.' Plainly, foreign visitors are nothing new to Woodstock.

Entertainments took place at the Manor House, and we hear of a performance of 'The Nigramansir (Necromancer), a morall interlude and a pithie, written by Maister Skelton, laureate, and plaid before the king and other estatys at Woodstoke, on Palme Sunday, 1501'. The play was printed by Wynkyn de Worde, but no existing copy is known.

The accession of Henry VIII (1509–47) brought many visitors to Woodstock, and in his youth the Manor was a scene of gaiety. He was a mighty hunter and a champion of all out-door sports, tilting, archery, and tennis. A tennis-court makes its appearance at Woodstock. He was a musician, a poet, and a patron of the new scholarship, whose Court was said to hold more true learning than the University itself. It was from Woodstock that he issued to the University of Oxford a command that the study of the Scriptures in Greek be included in the curriculum.

Henry paid several visits to the Manor House in the early part of his reign with Catherine of Aragon, the first of his six wives, and Cardinal Wolsey. From Woodstock Sir Thomas More dated a letter to his wife, and the sour visage of Thomas Cromwell enlivened the scene, especially for the Knights of St. John, who owned property in the town, for the Ladies of Godstow, and for the Chantry priests, all soon to be dispossessed. Here, too, the divorce of Catherine was discussed: a divorce that precipitated the mounting crisis between church and state, and the end of papal power in England. The ferocious old tyrant that Henry became in his later years did not frequent the Manor House, and it was greatly neglected.

Henry VIII dissolved the monasteries and replenished his treasury by the sale of their lands. In the reign of his sickly little son, Edward VI (1547–53), the chantries went the same way. There had been two chantry priests living in Woodstock, but from now on the inhabitants were left to the occasional ministrations of the Rector of Bladon, a situation from which Henry VI had thought to relieve them for ever.

In 1551 an inquiry into the state of Woodstock Manor was undertaken by three commissioners, who took evidence from a jury composed of 'ancient and discreet persons'. From this document we learn that the mansion itself had 'manie yeeres past beene decayed and prostrated', which is not, perhaps, surprising. In spite of the attention it had received from Henry VII, it had long passed the age at which buildings need constant repair, especially when largely unoccupied. It was never rebuilt, though James I made it habitable.

The document also mentions seven villages that belonged to the Manor: Hordley, Wootton, Coombe, Stonesfield, Hanborough, Bladon, and Old Woodstock. These are indifferently referred to as 'towns' or 'villages' although they were exceedingly small—Hordley now consists of one old house, the rest having disappeared, perhaps at the time of the Black Death. Many privileges of the inhabitants were stated, as well as the duties they were expected to perform: the tenants of Hanborough, Coombe, and Bladon had to cut the grass in the park; the tenants of Hordley had to sweep and clean the Manor House as often as the king chose to go there, and again after he left; to the tenants of Coombe fell the duty of cleaning the privies. As for the Lord of Stanton Harcourt, he had to find four men to cut browsing for the deer in winter-time, when the snow had lain on the ground for the space of two days. The call for browsers was given by the winding of a horn at the gate of Stanton Harcourt, and the king's bailiff who made the journey thither was to receive bread and cheese and a gallon of ale. The browsers, for their pains, had each a billet of wood as long as the handle of his axe, and as thick as he could carry on the edge of his axe to his lodging. But the lord of Stanton Harcourt himself had every year a buck and a doe from the king's park.

⚔ 7 ⚔

Edward VI was succeeded by his elder sister, Mary Tudor (1553–8), who had been brought up a Catholic, and had remained in that religion. Unfortunately, she was a bigot. Apart from burning 300 Protestants in four years, she brought England back for the time being under papal domination, and insisted on marrying Philip of Spain in the teeth of her subjects' opposition. When the Spanish marriage was projected, an insurrection broke out, with the object of deposing Mary in favour of her Protestant sister, Elizabeth. Sir Thomas Wyatt, the poet's son, was one of the leaders, but the plot failed. He was executed, and every effort was made to implicate Elizabeth. In March 1554 she was committed to the Tower. In May, feeling that the Tower itself was not safe enough, the queen ordered Sir Henry Bedingfield, with a large guard, to convey her sister to Woodstock. By Wheatley and Islip they came, the princess travelling in a litter, and we learn that there were foresters and keepers waiting at the park gates, and at the gate of the house six keepers 'weopened with forest bylls', a cheerful reception for the twenty-year-old princess.

We know already that the house was 'decayed and prostrated'. Four rooms had been prepared for her in that gatehouse which had been rebuilt by her grandfather and was probably the least dilapidated part of the mansion. Even so, the roof leaked, and, to the dismay of her jailer, there were only three doors in the whole house that could be locked and barred. It must have been an occasion of unrelieved gloom: Elizabeth, her life threatened, arriving at so desolate and ramshackle a place, unoccupied save by her jailers. She alighted from her litter and went to her lodging, a room with an arched roof of Irish oak, curiously carved and painted, 'after which tyme she sturred notte that nyght'.

The responsibility lay heavy on Bedingfield, and he suffered 'great disquiet' for the safety of his prisoner, 'in so large an house and unacqueynted countraye'. Tiles were replaced and windows were mended, but Bedingfield later complains of the sufferings of the guard during the long autumn nights, keeping their watch over 'thys house stondyng upon the hyll, sooe cold as yt doth'. So much for the prisoner's bleak outlook. She was strictly guarded: a hundred soldiers watched over the palace, sixty by day and forty by night. A system of espionage was established, and one at least of her favourite attendants was removed, to her great grief. But she never lost heart—though she is said to have wished herself a milkmaid—and she never believed that the charges against her would be proved:

> *Much suspected, of me*
> *Little proved can be,*
> *Quoth Elizabeth, Prisoner,*

she is said to have engraved on a window of the gatehouse. Her sojourn at Woodstock came to an end, for reasons which have remained conjectural, in the following spring. She was to return several times as queen, but no impression remains that Woodstock was one of her favourite residences !

In the first year of her reign Queen Elizabeth (1558–1603) con-firmed the Woodstock Charter, and later she gave the town four shops and thirteen cottages that had belonged to the Chantry of Our Lady, reserving to herself an annual rent of £4, which gave her the best of the bargain. Among these properties, the 'Woodstock Arms' and the 'King's Arms' have been identified, as well as some cottages in Brown's Lane, and others that used to stand in front of the church. She also granted a second weekly market on Fridays, and two more fairs of four days each at St. Nicholas and Lady Day. Such fairs were of great importance in bringing trade to the town. The Mayor was empowered to hold a court of 'Pie Powder' for the trial of offences at the fairs, and to have the profits arising from the weighing of wool and yarn brought to market, the weights used being those in force at Cirencester. At a later date Woodstock was made a staple for wool, which added to its importance and wealth. Tradition asserts that the loyalty shown by the people of Woodstock to the queen during her imprisonment was the cause of these benefactions.

There was trouble in the town about the middle of the queen's reign, caused by two quarrelling factions. In 1580 a constitution was drawn up, entitled 'Orders made, concluded, enacted, establishedd, and agreed uppon by . . . the Maior, Aldermen and Comon Counsell of the said Burrough for the quyet and civill government of

themselves and the Comynaltie of the same Burrough in the time of
William Skellton, Maior there'. If the Orders did not immediately
achieve their object, they tell us a great deal about the government of
Woodstock.

Since the days of the first Charter, the Corporation had become
an elaborate structure, with numerous officials. There was a High
Steward, Mayor, Recorder, six Aldermen, of whom one was Mayor,
twenty Common Councillors, Town Clerk, two Chamberlains, a
Cryer and a Sergeant-at-Mace. The Mayor, elected from the Aldermen by the freemen of the borough every Michaelmas, now received
a salary of £10, and sundry perquisites. The High Steward was
chosen from the more important gentry, and his few duties included
swearing in the Mayor. He was rewarded with a Christmas cake of
staggering size and content, and sometimes with a sugar-loaf. The
Recorder was the Corporation's legal adviser: a salaried official,
appointed by the Council, who was always made a freeman. He sat
beside the Mayor at the Sessions of the Peace and the View of Frankpledge. The Aldermen acted as Justices of the Peace. The Chamberlains received and paid out the town's money and were chosen from
among the Councillors. The Councillors themselves were voted upon
by the freemen out of a list submitted by the Corporation, but if
'mysliked' they could be dismissed by the Corporation alone. The
Town Clerk was a salaried official who advised the Mayor in the
Portmouth Court; he was a freeman of the borough and sometimes
a Justice of the Peace. Aldermen and Councillors had appropriate
gowns in which, preceded by the Mace, they were obliged to attend
the Mayor to Church on all high festivals. They were forbidden to
'revyle, miscall or gyve any unfitting, undecent or obprobrious
words' to each other under a penalty of 10s. Any member of the
public, reviling one of them, was liable to find himself in prison.

The freemen, on whom the whole constitution was based, no
longer formed a Merchant Guild, but kept a monopoly of trading
within the borough. Neither might a freeman employ a 'foreigner',
unless he had lawfully hired him for a year with the knowledge of the
Mayor. Freemen were, however, permitted to live outside the
borough and trade in it. For over two centuries a losing struggle
went on to prevent any but the freemen from trading in the town.

There were four ways of becoming a freeman: by birth, being a
descendant of the inhabitants enfranchised by Henry VI; by a seven
years' legal apprenticeship; by marrying a freeman's widow; or by
purchase, the Corporation bargaining for the best price they could
get. At a later date residents of substance were admitted to the

D

freedom, having 'paid their fees as gentlemen'. To sum up, the town was governed by the descendants of the chartered inhabitants of 1453, plus such new-comers as had qualified for freedom.

As regards the uproar going on in Woodstock at this time, which contrasted so strongly with a design for 'quyet and civill government': the protagonists in the affair were the Mayor, William Skelton, a licensed victualler, and George Whitton, a hot-headed and intractable member of the local gentry. One Owen Whitton had been Surveyor of the Manor and Park in Henry VIII's time, and George's father, another Owen, had been Mayor in the time of Edward VI. George himself, at the time the trouble started, was Surveyor of the Park, and had been an M.P. for the Borough, as well as Mayor. It seems clear that he wanted to rule the town, and to gain his ends, posed as the leader of a popular party, oppressed by the licensed victuallers, who, he declared, were 'confederate together' to foist themselves on the community. He 'riotously assembled' with his companions, marching about in armour, with 'long pyked staves, swords, bucklers, daggs and other monstrous weapons'. When the Mayor ordered them off, they threatened him and he was obliged to flee. Their shouts and outcries by night were 'the terror and admiration of the whole country inhabiting thereabouts'. At a mayoral election Whitton tried to 'shuffle the Mayor out of his place', and indulged in words and conduct the more unseemly that the election seems to have taken place in church. Displaced as an Alderman, he raised a riot in the High Street, making 'polts' with his mouth at the Mayor, and offering him a leg to put in the stocks. Other witnesses said it was the Mayor who lost his temper and raised a riot, as well may have been the case. It is a typical instance of the difficulty of controlling disorder in towns before the days of the police. The affair seems to have come to an indeterminate end, but Whitton continued for a long time to annoy his adversaries with lawsuits. The name of Whitton continues to crop up in Woodstock records for another 150 years, but none of George's descendants appear to have been so obstreperous.

Mention has already been made of the Portmouth, or independent borough Court. Offenders brought before it were, in most cases, summarily put in the stocks or pillory, or fined. Some, however, were committed to the Sessions of the Peace, where a full bench of magistrates sat with the Recorder. Most of the cases arose from drunkenness, quarrelling, and sheep-stealing. Sheep-stealers were committed to the Sessions and presumably hanged; vagrants were whipped, or, if they persisted, lost an ear, and were finally hanged.

Fines were imposed for selling or eating meat in Lent or on fast-days. Labourers desiring to move to another district had to have passes from the justices, lest they should be treated elsewhere as vagrants, such was the terror of every town that strangers would qualify for poor relief.

On the same day as the Sessions there was held in Woodstock a town meeting that went by the odd name of the View of Frankpledge. The name goes back to an ancient custom whereby the inhabitants of a place gave sureties for each other's good behaviour. In Woodstock, traces of the old function of the Frankpledge remained, but it had chiefly become a democratic meeting at which orders were made for the town's administration, such as the 'Order for quyet and civill government' already referred to. The Sergeant-at-Mace, under orders from the Mayor, summoned some of the freemen to serve as jurors, and the rest of the inhabitants to attend. Constables and ale-tasters were elected at this meeting, and fined if they refused the office; all matters affecting the town, its streets and markets, and the efficiency of its officers might be discussed. Anybody might lay a complaint before the jury. Disputes about property were settled, or complaints of 'forestalling' (buying goods before they reached the market) investigated.

In 1580 the View of Frankpledge made an order controlling the activities of glovers on market and fair days, from which we see that gloving had already become a Woodstock industry. Both Elizabeth and James I are said to have been presented with Woodstock gloves. The industry was not peculiar to Woodstock; it flourished in many towns and villages bordering the forests, which would suggest that the gloves were made from the skins of the deer that were hunted there. From now on, however, gloving becomes the chief of Woodstock industries, as it still is today. In the nineteenth century there were many small factories producing gloves, and though some of these were machine-sewn, far more were still sent out to be handstitched by women and girls in their own homes. It used to be a common sight in Victorian Woodstock to see women stitching gloves at the cottage doors, and skins hung out to bleach on the hedges.

But to return to Elizabethan Woodstock: it boasted another and very singular industry. This was polished steel-work, of such meticulous craftsmanship that the neckwear of an Elizabethan courtier was thus described:

> *His ruff did eate more time in neatest sitting*
> *Than Woodstock-worke in painful perfecting.*

The steel used was salvaged from old horseshoe nails, which, from contact with the road, had taken on 'a peculiar temper'. Beaten into small bars, it provided the raw material from which, with infinite skill, articles of great value were made. This industry reached the height of its fame in the eighteenth century, when a chain weighing 2 oz. was sold in France for £170. A Garter Star for the Duke of Marlborough cost 50 guineas, and a box in which to present the freedom of the borough cost £37. 16s. 2d. But by the middle of the nineteenth century Woodstock steelwork had ceased, killed by cheap imitations from Sheffield and Birmingham.

In 1595 died Richard Cornwell, a skinner of London, leaving £300 to found a grammar school in his native Woodstock; £100 for the house and £200 to purchase lands for the school and the master, 'whome I would have to bee a good preacher of the word of God', and £10 to pay for four sermons a year 'to the benefitt of the people', for ten years after his death. To carry out his bequest, the Corporation bought three houses in Oxford Street, and some other property. The school ran for centuries in a long room parallel to the Chancel of Woodstock Church, said to have been part of the Chantry property given by Queen Elizabeth to the town. In 1877, when the church was largely rebuilt, this room was destroyed, and the north aisle occupies its site. The school then moved to one of its three houses in Oxford Street, a house on the corner of Hensington Road, once known as the 'Pyed Bull', and now called the Old Grammar School.

One of the people whom Whitton had chosen to vilify was Sir Henry Lee of Ditchley, for many years Lieutenant of the Manor and Ranger of the Park, and in 1580, High Steward of the Borough. It was a choice that can scarcely have helped Whitton's cause, for Sir Henry, 'a gent of good estate and a strong and valiant person,' was on excellent terms with the queen, who used to visit his house at Ditchley, some three miles north of Woodstock. Sir Henry held, in the park, 'one lodge, "le highe lodge", with two gardens, and one "le woodyard", adjacent to the same, during his life'. He held three other lodges in the park, as well as 'one house called "Rosemunde" with one dovecot in ruins', and 'one house with a stable at the park gate'. Of all these, the chief was High Lodge, occupied by Sir Henry in the course of his duties at Woodstock. This ancient house is still standing, and is well worth a visit.

Crossing the bridge in front of Blenheim Palace we turn leftward where the road forks, leaving below us, near the edge of the lake, the spring called 'Rosamund's Well', on the traditional site of her 'Bower'. Farther on the road forks again, and we keep to the left,

dipping round the end of a narrow creek which the lake forms at
this point. The road now rises steeply, the eighteenth-century
landscape falls behind, and we reach an ancient park-land, a scene
of bracken, brushwood, and scuttling wild life, with here and there
a huge oak-tree, so incredibly ancient that it may well have seen

the Plantagenets riding to the chase. The sap, they say, still rises just
under the bark, and every spring these monsters put forth a few pale
leaves among their stiff, dead, scarecrow branches. Occasionally one
of them falls, a gigantic heap of rotten wood that quickly turns to
powder. Rounding a corner on top of the hill, we come upon High
Lodge, a battlemented stone building, which gives an impression of
age, remoteness and desolation. In the eighteenth century it still
boasted an iron gate, between stone pillars topped by urns, where
now is but a rickety wooden fence. From its flat-topped tower, if he
be lucky, the visitor may enjoy a magnificent view over Eynsham to
Wytham Woods, and away to the Berkshire downs, south of the
Thames.

High Lodge has another point of interest, for here, in the reign
of Charles II, died John Wilmot, Earl of Rochester, a Restoration
poet, of whom Dr. Johnson has written that he passed his life in 'an
avowed contempt of all decency and order, and a total disregard to
every moral, and a resolute denial of every religious obligation . . .
till at the age of one and thirty he had exhausted the fund of life and
reduced himself to a state of weakness and decay'. A native of
Ditchley and connected with the family of Lee, he was a favourite

HIGH LODGE IN 1950

of the king, who made him Ranger of Woodstock Park, and he was living at High Lodge when, it was said, the fear of death came over him. He repented of his evil ways, and died in 1680, 'in the bosom of the church he had rejected'.

8

Devoted to hunting, James I (1603–25), the son of Mary Stuart, revived at Woodstock some of the splendour of reigns long past. The condition of the Manor House was appalling, but the dauntless monarch had a few rooms fitted up for himself, and sent his household to cool their wrath under canvas in the park. 'The place is unwholesome,' wrote Sir Robert Cecil. 'It is unsavoury, for there is no savour but of cows and pigs. It is uneaseful; for only the king and queen, with the privy chamber ladies, and some three or four of the Scottish Council, are lodged in the house, and neither chamberlain nor one English councillor has a room.' The Union of the Crowns was not yet a union of hearts or Parliaments, and the English hated their poor, proud Scottish rivals for royal favour.

The Manor House was patched up during the next few years, judging by the visitors who were received there, and the festivities that took place. There was much coming and going between Woodstock and Ditchley, where the old house of Sir Henry Lee was hung with royal hunting trophies in the shape of stags' horns, and flat punning couplets that described the kill. In 1610 Henry, Prince of Wales, had a grant of the Manor, where two years later he entertained the king at 'one of the greatest and best ordered feasts that ever was seene'. There, too, George Villiers, later Duke of Buckingham, was created first Baron of Whaddon, 'with great ceremony, the king sitting upon his throne and the queen and princes being present.'

To the Corporation of Woodstock, the royal hunters would occasionally send presents of venison, which proved expensive to cook and eat in style. To consume a brace of bucks given by the Prince of Wales cost £6. 17s. of which £4 was for wine. The Corporation's wine-bill seems somewhat excessive, visiting preachers, for instance, being generously treated. 'For a quart of sack to Mr. Evans when he preached and dyned at Mr. Maior's, 12d.' In one year the cost of wine for preachers amounted to £1. 15s. 1d.

It may have been due to the number of visitors that came to Woodstock, but, between 1618 and 1635, the total number of licensed houses in the borough varied between fourteen and twenty-six, for a population of under 750. At one point the Mayor and Council resolved to reduce the number of ale-houses, as well as the 'immoderate strength' of the ale that was sold in them. Despite their good intentions, the total remained at about one ale-house for every fifty inhabitants. Licensed houses had to close at 9 o'clock in the evening and at service time on Sunday. No gambling was allowed in them, neither might a stranger stay unless he had given his name to the constables.

The reign of Charles I (1625–49) brought civil war to England, which ended in the temporary abolition of the monarchy, and the establishment, first of a Commonwealth government, and then of a Protectorate under Oliver Cromwell. In the very first year of Charles's unfortunate reign, he came to Woodstock to escape the plague, which was 'so violent in London, that at Woodstock, where the Court is, none may go from thence to return, nor any come thither, and for contraveners a gibbet is set up at the gate'. We are not told how many people were hanged on it.

The year 1634 gives us the first eye-witness description of the Manor House, written only a dozen years before the first stage in its destruction. Three gentlemen of the army at Norwich were passing

near, and one 'made bold to transgresse my rank', and visit the
famous mansion, the king not being in residence. He found it
'ancient, strong, large and magnificent', and sumptuous as well.

Our visitor passed through the gatehouse into the wide courtyard,
where a 'she gentle keeper' appointed her daughter to guide him.
He saw the great hall, spacious and 'church-like', divided by pillars
into aisles, and hung with tapestry. He saw the chapel of the Norman
kings, 'with 7 round arches, with 8 little windowes above the arches,
and 15 in them', a 'curious ffont' and a roof most admirably
wrought. Upstairs he saw the guard-room, the king's privy chamber,
which looked over the tennis-court into the town, and the king's
bed-chamber, with a view of the privy garden. He then visited the
queen's rooms, her guard-room and her chapel, which last he merely
describes as 'neat'. From the gatehouse roof he had a fine view of the
park, of 'lawns and waters', of High Lodge on its hill, and of other
handsome lodges 'wherein many gentlemen keepers of quality doe
reside'. Finally he saw the ruins of Rosamund's bower, with 'strange
winding walls and turnings', and the square paved well that is there
to this day.

The government of Charles I was intensely unpopular, and never
more than when he raised money by means which the mass of his
subjects thought illegal. The navy had been neglected under James,
and Charles's levy of 'Ship-money' for a good cause, but without
Parliamentary sanction, marked a definite stage in his downfall.
Woodstock, as one might expect from its history, was strongly
Royalist, and paid up its first levy with promptitude. Only seventy
people were assessed for the tax, the poor being exempt. The town
raised £20. 2s. 2d., of which eight persons had to find more than
half. In the following year the assessment was reduced to £15,
which was collected with more difficulty.

War between king and Parliament broke out in 1642. After the
Battle of Edgehill, in October, the Royalists reduced Banbury
Castle, and from thence marched through Woodstock to Oxford.
Oxford, as Royalist as Banbury was Parliamentarian, became the
king's headquarters, the seat of his government, and the refuge of the
Court. The Manor House was strongly garrisoned for the king, who
moved freely between Oxford and Woodstock, and enjoyed some
hunting. All around Oxford fighting was incessant, and as time went
on the Parliamentarian circle grew closer. Charles spent Sunday,
2 June 1644 at Woodstock, killing a brace of bucks. At supper, word
came to him that Waller's army, bent on his capture, was encamped
at Eynsham. He left that night and arrived back in Oxford early the

following morning. A feint attack on Abingdon drew off Waller, and in the evening Charles mustered his troops on Port Meadow and marched northward in the twilight, leaving his colours on the fortifications of Oxford. As dawn broke he crossed the Evenlode by Hanborough Bridge, and escaped between two armies of his would-be captors. At the end of the month he was able to return to Oxford.

The Manor House held for the king, but Waller passed through the town. Scorning to hunt, he demanded his pound of flesh in the form of fat bucks delivered to his quarters. No notice was taken, and a threatening letter descended on 'the head keepers and under-keepers of Woodstock Parke, or any of them ! If you faile to send the bucks, I shall not faile to fetch you, if you dare to lye in your houses !' Cromwell himself is said to have come into the town, and to have stayed at a house in the High Street that still bears his name and was once an inn. In June 1645 the king's forces were routed at the Battle of Naseby, and his cause never rallied. The Parliament men had but to capture Oxford and reduce the scattered castles and strong-points that still held for him.

In February 1646, 500 Parliamentarians came to plunder Woodstock, but the sentry gave the alarm and the garrison fell upon them. They got but a little loot from the houses and ten horses, eight of which were aged and 'destined to the dogges'. They fled with some loss.

The Manor House had been prepared for a siege. Captain Samuel Fawcett commanded the garrison, and had so strengthened the defences that it was thought fit to withstand a long attack. Garrison and townsmen dug together on the earthworks, which were still visible some 160 years later, and we hear that John Whitton 'laid out on the Park the sums which should have been for his children'. The ruins of Rosamund's Bower, with walls and pillars twenty feet high, were said to have been thrown down lest they should give shelter to the besiegers.

Woodstock was cut off from the garrison in Oxford by the beginning of April 1646, and the siege began about the 8th, the Parliamentarians 'battering that brave and ancient Manor-house with our ordnance', but so stout was its defence and so resolute the sallies made by its garrison, that it held out till the 26th, by which time not a barrel of powder was left. The Captain was resolved to leave his bones there, but the king sent commissioners to treat for a surrender, and what was left of the defenders marched out with the honours of war. The capture of Woodstock was treated by Parliament

E

as a victory, and the bringer of the news to the House of Commons received their thanks and £100. Next day the king left Oxford and took refuge with the Scottish army. The war, as it affected Woodstock, was over.

After the tragedy came the farce. In October 1649 the Commonwealth Commissioners came to take possession of the Manor. About seven of them, with their secretary, Giles Sharp, took up their residence in the half-ruined building, where they were assaulted by an energetic and resourceful poltergeist, which battered their persons as much as it alarmed their spirits. Royalist Woodstock accepted the story as one of simple supernatural interference, and the rector, Thomas Widdowes, wrote an account of it, entitled *The Just Devil of Woodstock*. The devil made imaginative use of very simple resources: a little gunpowder, tactfully placed; faggots of wood from the famous King's Oak, which the Commissioners had felled as being too monarchical; a black dog, three dozen wooden trenchers (used for meals between whiles), stones and glass from the wreckage, a warming-pan, some horses' bones, and a pail or two of 'green stinking water'. Billets of oak, stones, bones, glass, and furniture were flung dangerously about; gunpowder extinguished the candles or exploded in the fire; trenchers 'rolled horribly', or flew at heads; dogs howled and *Something* walked like a bear; loud bangs frightened the very poachers in the park; most horrible of all, a hoof was seen —by Giles—to strike a lighted candle. Such manifestations struck panic into Rumpish breasts, and the Commissioners, following the example of Mr. Speaker Chaucer in a happier mood, withdrew to Ewelme. At the Restoration the poltergeist was revealed as royalist Joe Collins, who, disguised as Giles Sharp, had planned and carried out the terror.

After the king's execution a survey was made of the Manor, which showed that the dilapidated building was even more extensive than had been suggested by the gentleman from Norwich. The great mass of rooms surrounded two courtyards, the second rather smaller than the first. A third, called the 'Pastery Court', was formed of kitchens and domestic offices, and there were outbuildings round the privy garden. 'The said house,' the surveyors declared, 'is much out of repaire, yett most of it fitter to stand than be demolished'. The 'brave and ancient Manor-house' had proved tougher than the ordnance of Parliament. It was to prove less tough than the first Duchess of Marlborough.

The mansion was sold to Lieut. General Fleetwood, Cromwell's son-in-law, and was stripped of most of its saleable materials, so that

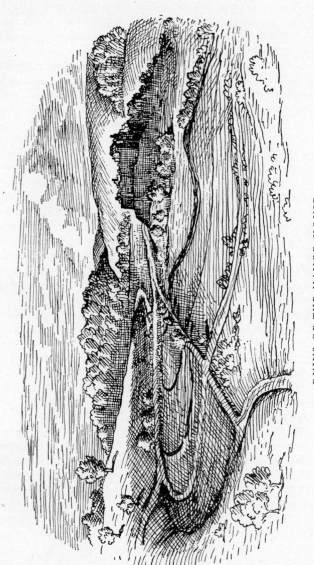

RUINS OF THE MANOR HOUSE

(After Dr. Plot's Print of 1677)

Anthony Wood, writing in 1659, described it as having already been pulled down, a gross exaggeration, as we know from Dr. Plot's print of 1677, and from the fact that, when Blenheim Palace was built in the early eighteenth century, a picturesque and still not hopeless ruin confronted it across the waters of the Glyme. The famous gatehouse was suffered to stand intact, and, after the Restoration, was occupied by Lord Lovelace.

Woodstock must have paid bitterly for its part in the Civil War. It had to find large sums for quartering Parliamentary troops, while its way of life, that had lasted so many centuries, was gone, it must have seemed, for ever. The life of the town had grown up round the Royal Manor, with the occasional visits of the Court, the comings and goings of important people with their retinues, the Rangers, high functionaries, and local gentry, who, in his absence, came to hunt the king's forest. The destruction of the monarchy brought distress for which no remedy was offered, since the Parliament men who bought the estates did not attempt to keep them up. The land was neglected, the deer sold, the timber carted away. Moreover, since the war, Oxfordshire had ceased to be a land of plenty in timber and corn.

The Cavaliers, as a class, 'went into cold storage', to emerge fairly intact at the Restoration, but individuals of moderate means suffered hardship from fines, or loss of preferment or office. Edmund Hiorne, the Town Clerk of Woodstock, who lived in Park Street in one of the Chantry houses that used to stand in front of the church, had given up the town armour to the royalist cause, an act for which he was forced to apologize on his knees at the Bar of the House of Commons before the Speaker, William Lenthall, a member for Woodstock, of which he had been Recorder. Hiorne was removed from office, and barely lived to enjoy his reinstatement after the Restoration.

The savage Puritanism of Cromwell's army accounted for much damage to Woodstock Church, and especially to its windows, which must have been exceptionally fine. In the west window had been figures of Henry V and his three brothers, kneeling, with the arms of England and France. Another window represented the story of Thomas Becket, of all saints the most revered, and closely touching Woodstock; while in another were the arms of Roet, Chaucer, and Burghersh, 'very old in glas'.

The Corporation mace dates from the Commonwealth. In 1655 the Mayor contributed £3, and the Council voted £10, plus the old mace, for the purchase of a new one. Five years later the new mace was remade, presumably with the object of adding the royal arms

and initials, and the crown. Also from this post-war period, in
Woodstock as elsewhere, consequent upon the shortage of small
coin, dates the issue of tradesmen's tokens, usually in the form of
farthings, which could be re-presented to the issuer in exchange for
goods or coin of the realm. This local coinage continued for twelve
years after the Restoration, and examples of Woodstock farthings
are said to be fairly common.

A new Corporation functionary appears, the Beadle of the Beggars
and Scavenger. Apart from minor street-cleaning, his duties were to
whip offenders when required, to drive children out of the church-
yard on the Sabbath, and dogs out of church during services. Later,
he was expected to keep beggars out of the town. His salary was
20s. a year, and his equipment consisted of coat, cap, shoes, stockings,
and wheelbarrow.

9

After the death of Cromwell and a general election, king and Parliament were restored as joint authorities by a people heartily sick
of extremes, and especially of Puritan repression. Wild were the
rejoicings that celebrated the accession of Charles II (1660–85).

In Woodstock a more normal state of affairs prevailed. Charles
took immediate steps to regain possession of his despoiled land, and
to stop the cutting of timber, which had already gone too far. He
added sixty acres of land to the Park, with a promise of compensation
to the tenants, which they had great difficulty in getting fulfilled.

Charles paid a flying visit to Woodstock, but the house was no
place to stay in for a monarch who respected his comforts. John
Evelyn, the diarist, passed through and 'beheld the destruction of
that royal seat and park by the late rebels'. He went on to Ditchley,
'an ancient seat of the Lees. . . . It is a low ancient timber-house,
with a pretty bowling-green. My lady gave us an extraordinary
dinner.' This was not the house that is standing there now. Charles
later became a constant visitor at Ditchley, for the reigning Lee,
subsequently Earl of Lichfield, married his daughter by the Duchess
of Cleveland. At Woodstock the great Earl of Clarendon, Chancellor
of the University, became Lieutenant of the Manor.

Shortly after the Restoration a royal commission composed of
county Cavaliers visited the borough, and 'deemed it expedient for
public safety' to expel from office several Roundhead officials,
including the Mayor, the Town Clerk, and a few councillors. This
action left its mark, and the Corporation took on an extremely Tory

and Jacobite complexion. It conferred on Titus Oates—who devised the story of the Popish Plot—the freedom of the borough, and failed to disenfranchise him when his perjuries were found out; it sent loyal addresses to Charles, and when James II came to the throne, the Mayor, Aldermen, and Town Clerk went to London at the town's expense with an address of congratulation.

In 1664 Charles II granted a new Charter under which the town continued to be governed for 222 years. In it the old Charters were confirmed, and sanction was given to the constitution we have seen adopted in 1580. Great was the activity of the Restoration Council. It cleaned up the streets and laid down stringent regulations for the markets; in the absence of the Rector, who still lived at Bladon, it busied itself with the affairs of the church, ordering new ceilings, changing the seating arrangements, and having the pulpit moved. The View of Frankpledge fined offenders for not playing their part in keeping the regulations, for not attending church, for holding dissenting 'conventicles', or for entertaining their relatives, contrary to an oppressive new law by which anyone who tried to settle in a new place could be sent back to the parish of his birth.

In 1686 Bishop Fell of Oxford determined that the Rector of Bladon and Woodstock should live in the more populous part of his parish. The Bishop spent £600 on buying and greatly enlarging an Elizabethan house. This he surrendered to the Mayor and Commonalty, to hold in trust for the Rector and his successors, that they might occupy it without paying rent 'or being at any charge other than keeping and leaving the premises in repair'. Should, at any time, the Rector not occupy the house, the rent was to go to the poor of Woodstock, until such times as the Rector might return. This only happened once, with a profit of £14 for charity.

So far, so good, but in modern times the charge of keeping and leaving in repair so aged a house became too great a burden, and as recently as 1949 the Rectory passed into the hands of the Church Commissioners, for its better preservation. It stands at the edge of the Park, overlooking the lake, and no house has a lovelier view from its windows.

In the seventeenth century there was a bell-foundry in Woodstock, on a site that has never been fully determined. The bell-founders were James and Richard Keene, who cast bells for Thame and Stow-on-the-Wold, but especially for Oxford, including several for Carfax Church. They seem to have operated between 1626 and 1686, at which latter date Richard, perhaps the son, appears to have been in charge.

In the summer of 1687 James II (1685–8) visited Woodstock in the course of a long royal progress. Macaulay says, 'he dined in state at the palace of Woodstock, an ancient and renowned mansion', but by all other accounts the place was a ruin, and the dinner must have been something of an *al fresco* affair. The Mayor and Corporation, less inured to royalty than of old, presented the king with '20 broad pieces of gold in a white sattin purse', and an address wherein they thanked him for the Declaration of Indulgence (which suspended the laws against Roman Catholics and Dissenters) and for his promise to protect the Church of England and the rights, liberties, and property of its members. In return, they pledged themselves to defend him and his government with their lives and fortunes against all comers. Two days later they surrendered their Charter to the king who, fortunately, had no intention of disenfranchising the borough, but merely granted a new charter in which the council was thrown open to Catholics and Dissenters.

The address which accompanied the satin purse followed the pattern of that presented to James by a number of towns, and it turned out to be a little premature, for the obstinate monarch proceeded to prove that he had no intention of protecting the Church of England, or even of governing his people according to their laws. By December 1688 the country was in revolt, and James fled across the Channel with his wife and infant son, leaving his subjects to greet as liberators his daughter Mary and her Dutch husband, William of Orange. One of James's last acts was to reinstate all charters the surrender of which had not been enrolled, and to annul those he had granted on such surrenders. In Woodstock his charter was not in force for more than a few months. In view of the fact that even royalist Oxford had flown the Orange colours in the High, it is noticeable that Woodstock greeted the accession of William and Mary with a sullen silence.

Among those who went to receive the new monarch on his arrival was John Churchill, a former member of James's own household, who some fifteen years later, as Duke of Marlborough and victor of Blenheim, was to have conferred upon him, by a grateful queen and nation, the honour and manor of Woodstock, together with Hordley, Wootton, Old Woodstock, Stonesfield, Coombe, Hanborough and Bladon, the hundred of Wootton and the park of Woodstock, 'and also all that demolished messuage, court house, or toft, with the appurtenances, together with the site thereof, now or formerly called Woodstock Manor-house'.

§ 10 §

The Woodstock Corporation, so active after the Commonwealth, in the eighteenth century went into eclipse. An element of self-seeking is manifest in all its actions, and before long we find the property of the borough being appropriated to the advantage of its officials. Nor was this peculiar to Woodstock. It was a disease which attacked the majority of public institutions at the time, not excluding the universities. The defeat of James II's attack on English law and custom had bred a feeling of security and confidence that was perhaps incompatible with integrity in public affairs. No fear of criticism from a higher authority, no thought of impending reform, troubled the placid waters of eighteenth-century self-satisfaction. The storm had been weathered once and for all; the institutions of England had proved themselves indestructible. To be old-established and possess an ancient Charter was to be unquestionably in the right.

In Woodstock this attitude of mind showed itself in a very practical way. Tenants of Corporation property were expected to find, in addition to their normal rents, contributions to the Mayor's Banquet. A leg of mutton here, a couple of rabbits there: a leg of pork from the 'King's Arms' and a 20-lb. rump of beef from what is now the post office. In 1715 some property in the present Rectory Lane was leased for a cockpit, on the understanding that the Common Councilmen should be at liberty to attend the matches free of charge. As to the Corporation Meadows (formerly 'le Pool'), instead of being let to the highest bidder, they were now apportioned among the Councilmen by lot; and if the lot fell to a Councillor who did not want it, he had to offer it to one of his fellows. This cosy arrangement lasted over a hundred years, into mid-Victorian times, when the meadows were again thrown open to competition, and rents rose with a bound.

The Mayor himself profited by the spirit of the times; his salary rose from 12 guineas in 1738 to £40 in 1807, not to be abolished till 1854. A typical entry in the Chamberlains' account-book runs: '1752. April 16. Paid to Mr. Cross at the Bear for the Mayor and gentlemen regaling themselves after a troublesome day's business £1. 3. 0.' On important occasions the Corporation feted the populace with cakes and ale, and themselves with something less homely. In 1803 a number of the inhabitants offered themselves as volunteers for the defence of the realm against Napoleon—a Home Guard, in fact. The Corporation arranged to form a body of Loyal

Woodstock Volunteers and opened a subscription list to defray
expenses. Characteristically, its own contribution was not money,
but beer to the value of £11. 1s. 8d. or about three hogsheads. And
this although, in 1835, when rents had risen after the Napoleonic
War, the total annual disposable income of the Corporation was
estimated at £140. In 1802 the Recorder resigned because 'my loss

THE MARKET CROSS

Destroyed in the 18th Century. (*After an 18th-century print.*)

of sight deprives me of the power of joining without inconvenience
in the festivities which accompany our annual meeting'—the View
of Frankpledge !

A gambling-fever afflicted the Council. In 1719 the Rector had
won a lottery prize of £1,000, which he applied to the use of the poor.
Between 1747 and 1755 the Council bought five lottery tickets,
hoping to pay for a new Town Hall, but they only lost their money.
The new Town Hall was finished, nevertheless, in 1766, and paid
for by the Duke of Marlborough, while the Council forked out
£3. 19s. 5½d. for an opening feast.

Few towns have suffered more than Woodstock from the loss of
ancient buildings, and the eighteenth century in particular took little

account of such memorials of the past. The stone Market Cross, referred to in 1279, had in the seventeenth century been furnished with arches supporting a roof to form a shelter. This became redundant when the Town Hall was built, since in its early days the ground floor of the latter was a market house, its entrances closed only by iron gates. The old shelter was accordingly torn down, cross and all.

Little better a fate has overtaken the church. In 1785 the north aisle was rebuilt in a style described by a contemporary as 'decorously and respectably simple'. It forms a melancholy contrast to the original south side. The new tower had been erected in the previous year and was, considered apart from the church, an unqualified success. It is difficult to judge of it now, for the stone balustrade which surmounted it had to be removed, for safety's sake, in 1948 and is still awaiting replacement. The tower has a set of chimes, which, until 1939, played a different tune every day of the week, but which, unfortunately, is no longer in use. Gone, too, since the last war, is the curfew that still rang every evening from October to March, reminding us of Woodstock's link with the Norman kings. In 1877 the church was ruthlessly restored; the Tudor Grammar School building was pulled down, the Corporation gallery torn out, and the building acquired its present aspect. One good thing emerged from the massacre: the fourteenth-century font, which had spent over a hundred years adorning a neighbouring garden, was restored to its rightful place.

The greatest loss of all was that of the Manor House. The first Duchess of Marlborough had quarrelled with Vanbrugh, her architect. He would have spared the ruin, but it came into her extraordinary mind that he intended to patch it up and live there. By her order the last vestiges of the Manor House were completely destroyed and the site levelled. Had it survived but another fifty years, it would doubtless have been there still, for the time was not far off when ruins were all the rage, and were actually built to romanticize a landscape. As it is the visitor, seeking a trace of that symbol of so much historic continuity, finds himself stumbling fruitlessly, knee-deep in nettles around a rabbit-warren.

The building of Blenheim Palace brought great changes to the borough. We have seen how a long succession of kings, occasionally occupying the Manor House, fostered the civic independence of Woodstock. From now on the monarchs came no more, while the permanent residence of Queen Anne's most powerful subject, and of his dynasty, could not be without its effect on the town's life. Nor

WOODSTOCK CHURCH IN 1946

would it have been possible to put back the clock and restore to Woodstock its tiny brilliance in the royal crown, for the conditions which had made it no longer existed. Neither the political position of the monarchy after 1688, nor the personalities of the Hanoverian kings, conduced to a Court that was the mainspring of national activity in the old English way.

Until the Reform Bill of 1832 the freemen of Woodstock, amounting to about 150, of whom many were non-resident, continued to return two members to Parliament. This seems all the more remarkable when we remember that the new thickly populated centres, such as Manchester and Birmingham, were not represented at all. The expenses of a Woodstock election in 1705 amounted to £105. 3s., most of which was laid out in hogsheads of ale, bread, cheese, and pipes for the freemen anywhere between here and London. In 1722, on the occasion of another election, no less than fifty-three neighbouring gentlemen received the honorary freedom of the borough, and, by this suspicious manœuvre, went on to the voting strength. By the Reform Act the town was deprived of one member, while the remaining one represented a larger district on a broader franchise. At the present day Woodstock forms a small part of the North Oxfordshire constituency, which includes the bigger towns of Banbury, Witney, and Chipping Norton.

The Corporation reached its lowest ebb in 1831, when the Recorder died. The Duke of Marlborough, as High Steward, claimed to nominate his successor, and was supported by some of the Council. The meeting at which the new Recorder was elected did not consist of the majority of the Council—attendance had for some time been falling off—and the Town Clerk protested against the illegality of the proceedings. After this both factions kept away from meetings, so that neither could elect a Recorder, and several meetings were attended only by the Mayor and Town Clerk. There was no View of Frankpledge, no election of Chamberlains, no proper nomination of Mayors, and no business of any sort transacted by the Corporation.

It is difficult to imagine the state of affairs in a town still protected from outside interference, when all internal administration had broken down, and it is not surprising that one of the inhabitants should have procured a writ of mandamus to compel the Council to meet. Meet they did in 1838, and as if by magic the evil spell was broken and the Council fell to its work with a will, as energetic a body as ever. They filled up the vacant places, swore in the bone of contention as Recorder, and took steps to put themselves on a

better footing. It is noticeable that while Woodstock was thus in
a state of chaos, the Municipal Corporations Act had been passed in
1835, providing a uniform constitution for all the boroughs to which
it applied, 'based on the model of the best municipal corporations'.
It did not, however, apply to Woodstock, which continued to be
governed under Charles II's Charter for another fifty years.

MARKET PLACE, WOODSTOCK, IN 1946

   Woodstock was still a market town at this time; it remained so,
in fact, until 1933. Its market day was Tuesday, the Friday market
granted by Queen Elizabeth having fallen into disuse. At the accession
of Queen Victoria it still had half a dozen annual fairs, the most
important being early in October, when cheese was the principal
commodity offered. We still have the October fair, but the business
is now done by roundabouts and coconut-shies. There were sixteen
licensed inns in 1822, including several coaching-houses, for, with the
improvement in the roads which began in the second half of the
eighteenth century, Woodstock had become a centre for coaching
traffic, and up to a dozen coaches passed through daily, to and from
London. The road to Oxford was still full of pot-holes, and high-
waymen were not unknown, but these considerations did not
discourage trips to public executions there, from all the surrounding

towns and villages: day excursions which included frequent stops for refreshment at the 'locals' on the way.

The mid-nineteenth century found Woodstock outwardly little changed. True, it was a good deal quieter, for the railways had become the recognized mode of travel and had ruined the trade of the road. The View of Frankpledge continued its regular meetings until 1853, but the Borough Sessions, formerly held on the same day, had long since fallen into disuse; in fact, during the fifty years before 1829, not a case had been tried. The same was true of the Portmouth Court, which in 1847 had come to an end, to be replaced by the new County Court. The freemen still held control of the Corporation, but their numbers had greatly decreased. As might be expected, very few hereditary freemen were now coming forward for admission and honorary freemen were being made to fill their places. The old machinery was gradually wearing out. In May 1886 took place the last Council meeting of the Mayor and Commonalty of New Woodstock under the Charter of Charles II. On 9 November of the same year their property passed to a new body, elected by the householders of a larger area under the Municipal Corporations Act.

Lack of space prevents us from pursuing this story into modern times, and indeed for a mere Introduction to Woodstock it has gone quite far enough. A great change has come over the town during the last few decades, with the coming of the motor-car, bus, and coach. The face and character of Woodstock have altered and seem to be altering every day. Mid-Victorian freemen would hardly recognize their home. Our shops are more numerous and Woodstock gloves still go all the world over, but our skilled craftsmen have dwindled in variety and number, and for many purchases we must take the bus to Oxford—a matter of half an hour. Gone are the blacksmith, the saddler, the chandler, the cooper, the potter, the tailor, the turner, the brewer, and the strawbonnet-maker. We have a larger population, but much of it works in Oxford. No longer do most Woodstock families occupy the same houses for generations; 'foreigners' move into them awhile and then drift on, leaving nothing but a feeling of impermanence. The Victorian peace has been shattered by the rapidity of modern transport. Our inns, newly Tudored, are bursting with life, as they were in the days of the stage-coach. Our streets teem with visitors, as they did when kings held Councils at the Manor House. Travellers between Oxford and Stratford-on-Avon pause to quench their thirst here, as doubtless Shakespeare did. The old stone-built town is fringed with modern houses, many neo-Birmingham, a few post-war utilitarian, still fewer that conform to the traditions of the place. One of the chief twentieth-century contributions to the lasting fame of Woodstock has been the arrangement and classification of the Borough Archives, and the provision of a muniment room in the Town Hall to accommodate them. The stage is all set for the writing of a full-scale history of Woodstock, which should surely be done. For the time may come when urban sprawl will devour what is left of the countryside, and Woodstock as a separate entity may disappear. Everybody who has known it will fervently hope not.

Thus times do shift; each thing his turn does hold;
New things succeed, as former things grow old.

PRINTED IN
GREAT BRITAIN
AT THE
UNIVERSITY PRESS
OXFORD
BY
CHARLES BATEY
PRINTER
TO THE
UNIVERSITY